BASICS OF
THEOLOGY

MICHAEL MCCULLAR

Smyth & Helwys Publishing, Inc.
6316 Peake Road
Macon, Georgia 31210-3960
1-800-747-3016
©2013 by Michael McCullar
All rights reserved.
Printed in the United States of America.

Library of Congress Cataloging-in-Publication Data

McCullar, Michael D.
Basics of theology / by Michael McCullar.
pages cm
ISBN 978-1-57312-672-4
1. Theology, Doctrinal. I. Title.
BT75.3.M327 2013
230--dc23

2013013456

CONTENTS

INTRODUCTION TO THEOLOGY

Mention the word *theology* and people automatically think of words like *hard, difficult and deep.* The formal study of theology is exactly that — hard, difficult and deep, — and is best left for professional theologians. So this will be an informal study of theology that will better prepare each of us to understand the basics of our faith. This study will also assist us in being better able to communicate our faith beliefs to others. It's one thing to believe in God, it's quite another to tell someone why you believe in God. Defending one's faith, or better put, explaining one's faith, is called *apologetics.* The defense isn't negative, as in arguing about religion; it's positive in that we can actually tell someone why we believe in a God we can't see, touch or hear. So, after this study you will be both a theologian and an apologist. You will have a much deeper appreciation for the issues of the Christian faith and be able to discuss the reasons you believe as you do. And, you will find that theology doesn't have to be scary, deep or better left to "*real*" theologians. Theology is for all believers and all believers should be experiencing theology. So let's proceed.

Theology is derived from the Greek words *theos* meaning deity and *logos* meaning word. Combined they form *theology* or, the *word of God.* We tend to see scripture as the Word of God, but the concept of the "word" is much broader than the Bible. In John we see Christ referred to as the *Logos,* the Word of God. Thus Christ is the embodiment of the Word, the Word made flesh and the Word in action. On a more personal level, each believer also functions as the Word as they live their lives. Thus theology covers the full landscape of faith, touching on virtually all facets of Christianity. In our study we will focus on the theology of God, Jesus Christ, the Holy Spirit, the Trinity, Salvation, Sin, Heaven and Hell.

Theology all and all Theology. But, we must begin with God. There is a temptation for contemporary believers to see Jesus as the main focus, but that would be counter-productive. All concepts in theology begin and end with God. Scripture begins with God in Creation and ends with the promises of his bringing it all together according to his purposes. In between the beginning and end are many elements that complete the study of God, but again, all theological study must begin with God.

Theology — the idea that one can speak a word (logos)
about the one God (theos) and thus come to an
understanding of the other realities of life

A. J. Conyers

GOD

God is at the dynamic center of all theological study, shaping both the definition and scope of theology. God is found at the beginning of all things created and promises to be the end all of life as we know it. But how do we know this? Do we believe because we learned to do so as children? If we asked ourselves exactly why we believe in God, would we respond, "Just because!" Being a believer who practices theology is more than assuming belief or following the lead of others. It is finding these truths in a personal way. It is personalizing your faith through a journey of self-discovery and seeking the ultimate truth. God is to be found and understood in ways provided through creation and the written Word. God is not abstract and unfathomable. He is both personal and approachable, and wants us to view him in those exact ways.

When one sets out to prove the reality and existence of God it is best to begin with scripture. Kendall states that the truth about God is to be found in God's revelation of himself and his truth. Grudem believes people have an inner sense of God and have both scripture and nature as proof of God's reality. Scripture is a public record gathered throughout history of God's actions and purposes. Scripture never attempts to prove God, in fact, scripture ignores the question altogether. Scripture assumes the pre-existence of God... "*In the beginning God*"...and builds from that understanding the revelation of God's purposes. Evans writes: "It does not seem to have occurred to any of the writers of either the Old or New Testaments to attempt to prove or argue for the existence of God. Everywhere and at all times it is a fact taken for granted."

Scripture can be used as a tool to provide for the reality and existence of God. No doubt about that, but is there more than scripture to further form our theology of God? Yes, and, quite possibly, it's an argument as strong as the Bible, yet one more personal in nature can be found within each of us. It is believed by most theologians that humankind was created with an inner sense of God, of something bigger than they have capacity for. Blaise Pascal describes this inner-sense as a "God-sized hole" in each person that can only be filled through a relationship with God.

> We know the truth, not through our reason but also through our heart. The metaphysical proofs for the existence of God are so remote from human reasoning, and so complex, that they have little impact. Even if they were of help to some people, this would only be for the moment during which they observed the demonstration, because an hour later, they would be afraid that they had deceived themselves (Pascal).

The *soul* is the essence of Pascal's belief. Each person is born with a soul, and it is that part of us through which God interacts. A soul not reconciled with the Creator is a restless spiritual entity that will never know lasting peace. Attempts will be made to rectify the void, but all attempts will fail in the long run. The soul occupies the portion of humankind that is reserved for God. People remark, "I know God is real because I feel him in my heart." The heart is often symbolically referred to as a place of spiritual and emotional feeling. Another phrase used today to refer to the spiritual space within each person is the "dynamic center" of one's life. Each and all point to the inner-reality of God felt by those who are open to the Creator God.

Unfortunately, there are millions of people who are not open to the inner realities of God. They would cite such inner-feelings as being desired by the individual and not originating from God. For those suffering from skepticism exists the argument by nature: the belief that the universe and all things within cry out for the reality of God. Psalm 19 records the reality of God's creation: "The Heaven's declare the glory of God and the firmament proclaims his handiwork." The moon, sun, stars, skies and earth all put forth ample evidence of the reality of a creative God. "Look up, look around, and tell me you do not see God in all of this," one might declare. Yet some people are not swayed by nature, citing instead the Darwinian approach of process evolution, the Big Bang theory, and "it just started with ooze and the next thing you know...!"

For those who ask for even more material proof that God exists and is behind all creation, there exists formal arguments that delve much deeper than those already dealt with. The following are short synopses of the formal arguments for God's reality.

COSMOLOGICAL: This argument considers the fact that every known thing in the universe has a cause. Therefore, it reasons, the universe itself must also have a cause, and the cause of such a great universe can only be God (Grudem). *Kosmos* is the Greek word for *world* with an inferred focus on orderliness, specifically in contrast to chaos. The astounding order of all things suggests a First Cause, since nothing we see is its own cause. This First Cause, or the power behind the initial existence of all things, is God.

TELEOLOGICAL: *Telos* is the Greek word for *goal* or *purpose*. This argument focuses narrowly on the design, harmony, and purpose of all things in existence. Since the universe was apparently designed with great purpose and exists in harmony, a purposeful and intelligent designer must have been behind it all. Theology considers this intelligent and purposeful designer to be God. This argument has been vigorously attacked by those who have made evolution a scientific principle and who see great coincidence in the existence and order of the universe. While it remains *en vogue* to see science as the end all explanation for all existence, theology's response continues to be based on the profound complexity of mankind. "Mankind operates with a depth of intelligence, creativity, moral awareness, self-consciousness and God-consciousness that demands an explanation that Naturalism (evolution) seems powerless to provide" (Urban).

A theological response from science is an even more convincing argument for a God of creation:

According to Paul Davies, the odds against randomly generated initial order are staggering: If the universe is simply an accident, the odds against it containing appreciable order are ludicrously small. If the Big Bang was just a random event, then the probability seems overwhelming that the emerging cosmic material would be in thermodynamic equilibrium at maximum entropy with zero order. As this was clearly not the case, it appears hard to escape the conclusion that the actual state of the universe has been chosen or selected (Weaver).

An example that is easier to understand than the one above was presented by William Paley. His now famous line is this: "A watch calls out for a watchmaker." His view is that a watch with intricate parts that work in unison and precision did not just "appear;" a watchmaker was behind it all. He goes on to say, "the watchmaker is to the watch as God is to the universe." Hard to imagine this ordered universe coming into existence by happenstance. That would be even more miraculous than Creation itself.

MORAL: This position bases the reality of God on the seemingly inherent sense of right and wrong, and base level morality found in people. Colin Brown in *Exploring the Christian Faith* writes, "The Moral Argument claims that, whether people acknowledge it or not, their sense of moral values points to the existence of a personal, moral Creator, who has built into our moral make-up a sense of justice and obligation to others." Those who point to an evolved existence outside of a creator God see basic right and wrong and morality as societal, and cultural creations that are learned, not bestowed. Theology counters that either our moral make-up tells us something about the nature and purpose of reality (points us to God) or they are meaningless. Plus, on a common sense level, if morality was truly happenstance, coincidental and learned, from whom did it spring initially? It obviously had to begin at some point through someone.

BOTTOM LINE: Theology is at its simplest the study of God. There are many reasons that people accept the reality of God. A unique inner-sense of God's touch is common to believers, as is the reality of God in all things created. While scripture never attempts to prove God's existence, it in effect does just that. It is a convincing history of God's purposes played out in and through creation. However, for one not inclined to believe, scripture is not the answer to the riddle. The above formal arguments exist for the skeptical and for those who are faith-impaired. Bottom line is this: God is not something to be proven. The most convincing argument is just that, an argument, and not substantive proof. God seems to have designed it this way. Theology isn't based on proof; it is based on faith.

You are the most hidden from us
and yet the most present amongst us.

Augustine

SCRIPTURE

The word "Bible" is derived through Latin from the Greek '*biblia*' (books). The Bible is unique among historical writings as it is seen to be inspired, even commissioned by God. It is a collection of 66 books or letters in two major sections; the Old Testament and the New Testament. *Testament* is most often translated in Greek from Latin as *Covenant*, so in essence we have the Old Covenant and the New Covenant.

Scripture as we know it wasn't simply handed down by God on tablets *à la* Moses and the Commandments. Canonization was required in order for a book or letter to be accepted as meriting inclusion into scripture. The word *canon* was used by Greeks to mean a measuring of some type. As time progressed, the meaning shifted to encompass "standard" and "norm." The process of canonizing scripture was a lengthy one that took centuries and was fraught with much debate. Many writings were considered for inclusion but were deemed inappropriate or simply didn't measure up to the desired standards. Others were finally included, but faced vehement opposition during the process of review and judgment. Two prominent New Testament letters that barely made the cut were James and Revelation. James was said to be too practical and lacking in references to Jesus, and Revelation was, well, it was Revelation and greatly unique.

Old Testament books began through oral traditions as early as Abraham (1800 BC), with the first written portions being laws, poems and songs dating from the Exodus (1300 BC). It wasn't until the Council of Jamnia in AD 90 that the Old Testament was officially canonized. This was during a prolific period of writing by Christians, so Jews effectively drew a line between Hebrew writings and those of the new movement.

The New Testament came together in a much shorter time span, but the process was much more difficult and fractious. For approximately 30 years after the death of Jesus, there were no written accounts of his life or teachings. The Hebrew practice of oral accounts was widely utilized until the AD 50s when formal writings began to appear. It wasn't until the 4th century that the New Testament as we know it came together. This process was accomplished at various councils as the canonization process was completed.

APOCRYPHA: Many people are aware that the Bible used by the Catholic Church contains additional writings and is therefore much longer than the Protestant Bible. The Catholic version includes the Apocrypha, a collection of books that were not deemed as worthy of canonization in the 4th century. The additions were made to the Catholic version of scripture in AD 1546 at the Council of Trent, as a reaction against the Protestant Reformation led by Martin Luther. This move effectively split Christianity into two distinct divisions, Protestants and Catholics, with two versions of scripture.

BIBLICAL INSPIRATION: Since the Bible is often referred to as "the Word of God," it is easy to view scripture as being both empowered and inspired by God. This is quite a feat considering there were many contributing writers but only one author of scripture. This type of inspiration is called "plenary" inspiration, a process whereby God superintended the writings of scripture as it was being recorded. In *Exploring the Christian Faith,* Walter Moberly defines scriptural inspiration this way:

> The Bible is distinct and special because it is inspired by God. And although the actual word 'inspired' is used only once in scripture itself, the idea of inspiration is basic to the whole of it. God took the initiative in giving us the Bible. He took the lead in revealing himself in history, in giving his people a right understanding of his revelation, and in providing that a permanent and

reliable record of all this should be made. The authority of the Bible is not simply the authority of eminent people, but of God himself.

The inspiration of scripture not only validates the Bible; it also provides assurances that what we possess is all we need to fully faith God. 2 Timothy 3:16 reads, "All Scripture is given by inspiration of God, and is profitable for doctrine, for reproof, for correction, for instruction in righteousness." Thus, Scripture contains all we need for understanding our faith, for creating a lifestyle of faith and right-eousness, and for discerning correct theology and teaching. Divine inspiration makes the Bible an all-inclusive book of faith.

Sadly skirmishes have broken out through the years over other descriptive words for the Bible. *Infallibility* is one word that some have insisted must preface any reference to scripture in order to con-firm the unfailing nature of the Bible. That the Bible is a document that can be trusted to not fail seems to come with the package. The title "Word of God" should indicate a level of trust and comfort that the Bible is unique to an all powerful God.

Inerrancy is easily the most contested descriptive word of all time used to describe the nature of scripture. Those who insist on citing scripture as inerrant, or without any measure of error, are uti-lizing a term that scripture itself doesn't contain. Defined properly, "inerrancy means that scripture contains neither errors of fact (material errors) nor internal contradictions (formal errors)" (Brown). Obviously, there are errors related to dates and locations in scripture, as well as proven cases of scribes adding a bit of their own wisdom and preference along the way. A case in point is the last few verses of Mark that were undoubtedly added by a scribe during a process of translation. Matthew also adds a caveat to the teaching of Jesus on divorce that the other writers did not include. Mistakes? Errors? Problems? Well, yes, there are a few mistakes or contradic-tions involved, but with oral tradition and loosely written accounts handed down for centuries, what else should be expected? God chose to use real people and, along the lengthy way, these real people did what real people do — they erred a bit here and there. Do a few misplaced dates, locations, or mis-quoted items lessen the credibility of scripture? The answer is an emphatic no. In no way, form, or fashion is scripture lessened or diminished due to a few clerical issues or dates that were misrepresented. The Bible is the Word of God pure and simple, and because of that fact, no other descriptive language needs to be used as a qualifier.

VERSIONS: One might inquire as to why there are so many versions of the Bible in print today. For decades, even centuries, there was the staple King James Version in use by the majority of believers. That famous version was authorized by the namesake in 1607 in order to provide the Church of England a more precise, direct translation of the Bible from the Greek and Hebrew. The King James Authorized Version was not the first translation into English intended for the common person. An early scripture used by the Catholic Church was the Latin Vulgate (AD 400), written in a language that was hardly spoken in the 16th century. Prompted by the Protestant Reformation several translations were completed, providing a common language Bible that any person could use. Of the several translations predating the King James Version, most notable were versions by John Wycliffe, William Tyndale, Miles Coverdale, and Thomas Matthew. In 1611 the authorized version commissioned by King James was completed in Oxford and was provided to the people. Since that time a number of translations have become available, each an improvement on the 1611 version. Today there are more options available than at any time in history, and most are excellent translations from the original languages.

pasa graphe theopneustos
(All Scripture is God-breathed)

JESUS

The theology of Jesus of Nazareth is centered in the New Testament. Therein lies the story of his spectacularly unique birth, his early childhood and his earthly mission and ministry. To focus on Jesus is to entertain a complex and deeply theological figure. Jesus embodied both humanity and divinity simultaneously, being both fully human and fully God. No one before him and no one after him existed as he did. In fact, no one else was born to a virgin mother, lived sinlessly despite enduring multiple temptations, became the prophesied Messiah, died yet resurrected, and later ascended to heaven before witnesses. The person of Jesus is so complex that theologians have debated portions of his life for centuries. Leaving the debates to the professionals, we will center our attention on the major elements of his existence that shape our basic theology.

BIRTH

The unique birth of Jesus is described in detail by both Matthew and Luke but neglected entirely by John and Mark, as well as all other New Testament writers. Even in Matthew's extensive account, questions have arisen concerning dates and time in history. Matthew lists Augustus decreeing a worldwide census that prompted Mary and Joseph to travel and to be registered. Historical record shows that Emperor Augustus never registered the entire Roman Empire, much less the whole world. Matthew cites a census occurring while Quirinus was Governor of Syria (Luke 2:22), but his reign would have placed Jesus at eight years old during such a census. Matthew also has Herod ordering all children two and younger to be killed, and has Wise Men from the East involved in the birth sequence. Luke mentions neither Wise Men, Quirinus nor Herod, and has shepherds participating in the birth.

Wouldn't it seem that the birth of the Messiah would be worthy of more coverage, and, at the very least, more consistent reporting? How could Matthew have missed the date of a census by eight years? Why did the other New Testament writers ignore the birth altogether? It is best to not make too much of these issues and discrepancies. It wasn't uncommon in first century literature for dating to be an afterthought. John and Mark must have been so comfortable with the unique birth of Jesus that they passed over it and progressed to other times in his life. Theologically, it's important to focus on the fact that the Messiah was born in ways both divine and human, and not as important to focus on exact dates and visitors to the event.

The deepest theological implications are to be found in the virginal conception and/or virgin birth. The human mother of Jesus conceived through the Holy Spirit and her pregnancy was profoundly supernatural. Grudem sums up the theological significance of the supernatural conception:

1. It shows that salvation must come from the Lord, a divine act, and never through human effort.

2. The virgin birth made possible the uniting of full deity and full humanity in one person.

3. The virgin birth makes possible Christ's true humanity without inherited sin.

While the sinlessness of Jesus is central to theology, it has nevertheless spawned much controversy among scholars, theologians and philosophers. Roman Catholics deal with the sinlessness of Jesus by saying that Mary was sinless due to her conception. Protestants find absolutely no scriptural basis for this view and have roundly dismissed it over the years. It seems that scripture adequately deals with the sinlessness issue by detailing the uniquely supernatural aspects of the conception. In Luke 1:35 we read, "The Holy Spirit will come upon you, and the power of the Most High will overshadow you; therefore the child to be born will be called Holy, the Son of God." With the use of "Holy" (having to do with both righteousness and separateness) and the detail of God's activity and involvement level, it can be held that the lineage of sin was broken or superseded by divine action. Therefore, the sinlessness of Jesus had everything to do with God and nothing to do with either of the earthly parents.

DUAL NATURES

Jesus is seen as having had two distinct natures while on earth. As demonstrated through the virgin conception and the interaction of the Holy Spirit, Jesus was both fully human and fully God. Several scripture texts deal with the dual natures of Jesus: Is. 9:16; Jer. 23:6; Micah 5:22; Jn. 8:40; Acts 2:22; Rom. 5:15; I Cor. 15:21.

The concept of an actual person holding both full humanity and full divinity is mind-boggling and impossible to fully comprehend. It is easily chalked up to the "mysteries of God" category and simply taken on faith. While the "how's" will never be fully understood, the "why's" are much easier to fathom.

> Any attempt by ordinary man to imagine God results in nothing but the vague oblong blur complained of by those modern people who make the attempt. Yet if man can see God focused and be convinced that he is seeing God, scaled-down but authentic, he can...add all the other inklings and impressions that he has of the majesty, magnificence, and order of the Infinite Being, and see God... It is a fascinating problem for us human beings to consider how the Eternal Being—wishing to show men His own Character focused, His own Thought expressed, and His own Purpose demonstrated— could introduce Himself into the stream of human history without disturbing or disrupting it. There must obviously be an almost unbelievable scaling-down of the size of God to match the life of the planet. There must be a complete acceptance of the space-and-time limitations of this present life. The thing must be done properly—it must not, for example, be merely an act put on for man's benefit (Phillips).

Connor sees Jesus as the fitting end result of creation's aim, as the mediator between a loving God and the tainted created people. "God has no relations with the world, either creative or redemptive, except through Christ as the agent of His outpouring energy and power." Is Connor saying that God cannot have a direct relation to His created people? That would seem to lessen God in many ways. No, I think he is stating that God chose to relate redemptively with humankind through Jesus. This being so, then this explains why Jesus came to earth in human form and lived out life as He did.

Another rationale is found in the Old Testament story of Moses. Picture Moses kneeling in the vicinity of the burning bush. God's revelation was too powerful for Moses to endure for any length of time, thus the changing of his countenance. Plus, God communicating as/in a bush that seemed to blaze wasn't fully relatable. But God coming in human form allowed for full accessibility and relatability that could be embraced by any and all people.

> When Holy Scripture speaks of God, it does not permit us to let our attention or thoughts to wander at random. When Holy Scripture speaks of God, it concentrates our attention and thoughts upon one single point and what is to be known at that point. If we ask further concerning the one point upon which, according to scripture, our attention and thoughts should and must be concentrated, then from first to last the Bible directs us to the name of Jesus Christ (Barth).

MESSIAH

The title "Christ" is Greek and is derived from the Hebrew word detailing the Old Testament expectation of a coming Messiah. The root meaning of this word is "One who has been anointed." The Hebrew practice throughout history was to have anointed kings, specially called out for service by God. As time progressed, that mindset became synonymous with the anticipation of the Messiah as an anointed King. The idea of a coming "second David" was common among latterday Hebrews and was kindled by fervent nationalistic desires. The idea was also present that the Messiah would come from within Israel, a new David rising through the ranks. This rampant mindset was exactly what made Israel see Jesus as a suspect-Messiah from the beginning. Jesus was antithetical in every way to the anticipated Messiah, one who would be more political than religious. While the Hebrews weighed their messianic desires on earthly needs, Jesus came in ways that were diametrically opposite:

> Jesus saw it as his calling to play a unique and definitive role, namely to intervene on God's behalf and to resolve the conflict between divine faithfulness and human unfaithfulness. Jesus saw himself as Israel's representative, as the obedient man in whom the covenant would be made firm. He knew himself chosen by God for that purpose, and more than that, expressly sent by him. In him Israel's way is now being fulfilled and so the blessed rule of God breaks its way through the world (Berkhof).

Berkhof makes an astoundingly powerful theological statement in the paragraph above that literally sums up the messianic role of Jesus. "In him Israel's way is now being fulfilled..." In Jesus, the primary role of Israel as God's chosen group to reconcile the world/creation back to Him was completed. Israel was to function as a "holy nation and a nation of priests," a group committed to reaching the world (all peoples) for God. Israel drew an incomplete grade on this assignment (some would argue a failing grade) and left much of God's work unfinished. Jesus as Messiah created a permanent route for God's created peoples to return to Him for salvation, purpose and relationship.

JESUS as LOGOS

This concept of "logos" is central to theology, especially the theology of the Trinity, yet it is confusing to most believers. While logos essentially means "word," John was using an expanded meaning when he defined Jesus in 1:1. Hebrew thought saw the "word" as defining a reality of God as distinct, active and purposeful. Greek thought expanded the Hebrew definition to mean "a principle of holding all things together." Thus God is seen as the cohesive force of creation that provides unity, reason, and cohesion to all creation. By John defining Jesus as Logos, he is defining him as God. Believe it or not, this was a huge step in first century theological thought (John was the only writer to present Jesus as Logos), but a greatly necessary step nonetheless. By presenting Jesus as Logos, John was portraying the incarnation and preexistence in a single word. This statement is pivotal to all theology pertaining to Jesus: "Jesus not only spoke God's word; he was the Word of God, and that incarnate" (Garrett).

JESUS as SON OF DAVID

When Jesus was called Son of David it signaled an obvious retrospective of Israel's wish for a Davidic messiah. Jesus did fall into the lineage of David, yet he did not fulfill the messianic role historically associated with David. II Samuel 2 provides a common Hebrew view of a future deliverer, one who is eternally linked with David. It is used in the New Testament to denote Jesus being of the lineage of David as the "goal of Old Testament salvation history" (Goppelt). Primarily the description was used to influence Hebrews toward viewing Jesus as the true Messiah, and one that did fit the prophecy of the Old Testament.

JESUS as SON OF MAN

Jesus referred to himself most often as the Son of Man. This title is used eighty-four times in the first three books of the New Testament, always by Jesus in reference to himself. In Old Testament writings the term was used as a synonym for humanity (Ps. 8:4). Most theologians see the term Son of Man as best identifying the human element of messiahship and focusing on the full humanity of Jesus' dual natures.

JESUS as SON OF GOD

References to Jesus as Son of God were the most theological titles used for him by New Testament writers. However, this title caused numerous problems for the practicing, orthodox Hebrews.

> ...according to the New Testament narrative, it was this title, or rather the claim to this title, which was the principal charge against Jesus in the eyes of the orthodox Jewish authorities. When Jesus spoke of My Father, as John tells the story, This made the Jews still more determined to kill him, because he was not only breaking the Sabbath, but, by calling God his own Father, he claimed equality with God (John 15:17-18) (Barclay).

A primary presentation of Jesus by the New Testament writers' as Son of God was done to promote the full Deity of Jesus. While Son of Man pointed to the human element of Jesus' dual natures, Son of God proclaimed Jesus as equal to God and fully Divine.

This title was obviously problematic for the Jews, but was of great interest to Gentiles who saw in Jesus many God-like attributes. Plus, it is this title that gave Jesus the "right" to perform miracles and to speak for God. Not that he needed humankind's permission to speak for God, but it was necessary to provide an entree into the minds of mere mortals. By claiming to be the actual Son of God and by performing miracles, Jesus gave Gentiles more opportunity to believe than to not believe.

DEATH of JESUS

The synoptic writers tell the story of the trial, sentencing, torture, crucifixion, death, burial, resurrection and ascension of Jesus in remarkably stark manners. Jesus had become an enemy of the elite Orthodox Jewish leaders who rejected his claims of messiahship and saw him as blasphemous. While he was but a minor concern to Rome, the Jews found ways for Rome to be involved in ridding them of their worrisome Rabbi. After successfully having Jesus tried, convicted and sentenced to die, the Jewish leadership were no doubt overjoyed that he would be killed in the most ignominious of ways: by crucifixion. "This form of execution, which originated with the Persians, is rarely used by the Greeks, but is much employed by the Romans. It is considered not only particularly dreadful but also shameful, for it is meted out only to slaves and non-Romans convicted of murder, piracy, treason and rebellion" (Spoto).

Jesus spent less time hanging on the hewn wooden cross than most who were sentenced to die in that manner. Attached to the cross by spikes driven into the hands and feet, one was expected to hang for long periods, with death finally coming by suffocation. As was the life he lived before the cross, Jesus was unique even in his death.

JESUS as SALVATION

Theologically, the death of Jesus is foundational to all of the Christian faith. It is with his death that the salvation of humankind takes shape. "The Lord has laid on him the iniquity of us all" (Is. 53:6); "...the Lamb of God, who takes away the sin of the world" (Jn. 1:29); "Christ redeemed us from the curse of the law by becoming a curse for us, for it is written: 'Cursed is everyone who is hung on a tree'" (Gal. 3:13); "He himself bore our sins in his body on the tree, so that we might die to sins and live for righteousness; by his wounds you have been healed" (1 Pt. 2:24).

The common term for Jesus bearing the sin penalty is "propitiation." Grudem defines propitiation as "A sacrifice that bears God's wrath to the end and in so doing changes God's wrath toward us into favor." A major question facing theology is "at what point was the sin penalty paid?" Jesus was perfect and without sin, so how did he bear the sin penalty for humankind without sacrificing his perfect sinlessness? Some see the actual moment of death as the defining moment of the sin-payment, while others see Jesus calling out, "My God, my God, why have you forsaken me?" (Matthew 27:46) as the time of penalty-payment. It would certainly seem that Jesus would have, at some point, borne the cumulative sin burden of all people. For this to happen, a lapse between God the Father and God the Son would be necessary for the payment to be made. Since God cannot be of sin, a separation would need to occur for Jesus to take the burden on himself. Is it then that Jesus actually gave up his divine nature for some period of time in order to accept the human sin penalty? This does seem to be the case in order for full salvation to be an option.

RESURRECTION of JESUS

As scripture states, "on the third day" Jesus resurrected from the dead. This resurrection from the dead actually completed the salvation provision of God the Father through Jesus the Son. It's one thing to bear the sin penalty for a moment in time; it is quite another to put the penalty to rest for all eternity. In defeating death, Jesus also defeated the eternal power and possessiveness of sin. Never again would debilitating sin have full power and control over humankind without humankind's consent. The power and possibility to overcome sin and its negative spiral was secured by the death and resurrection of Jesus.

It should be of no surprise that the centrality of the resurrection to faith has led many to dismiss it as a genuine event. Great pains have been taken to negate the reality and/or necessity of the event. However, without the resurrection, there is no salvation. Thiessen sees the resurrection as pivotal to the authenticity of Christianity in three main areas: (1) All teaching and belief in Christ would be misplaced if the resurrection were not true; (2) It is foundational to the act of salvation; and (3) It is important to the validity of all prior miracles. Paul writes, "But if it is preached that Christ has been raised from the dead, how can some of you say that there is no resurrection of the dead? If there is no resurrection of the dead, then not even Christ has been raised. And if Christ has not been raised, our preaching is useless and so is your faith" (1 Cor. 15:12-14).

Despite the fact that the resurrection is so central to Christianity that without it the movement is flawed to the foundation, it still takes a great amount of faith to believe it occurred. People simply aren't accustomed to the dead coming back to life. However, seen in connection to all prior miracles (including the virginal conception), the resurrection of Jesus simply confirms and completes God's plan. No miracle stands alone in God's overarching plan; they all connect to the miracle of all miracles, the resurrection.

There is no atonement except with blood

Hebrews 9:22

Therefore God also highly exalted him and
gave him a name above every name.

Philippians 2:9

HOLY SPIRIT

The Holy Spirit is that portion of the Godhead that is easily the most mysterious in both function and structure. The Holy Spirit is seen as operating behind the scenes, in supernatural and ethereal ways. Even the Hebrew word for *spirit* lends to the supernatural nature of the Holy Spirit, meaning *breath* and *wind*. The translators of the King James Version also added to the fray by translating *Spirit* as *Ghost*.

A mistake in theology would be to distance the Holy Spirit from the work of God as Father and God as Son. They are eternally linked and cannot be separated in equality, only function. At times, the work of the Holy Spirit directly intersects the role or function of God the Father or God the Son, effectively going beyond a tandem relationship. A case in point would be the Holy Spirit taking over much of the earthly ministry activity after the ascension of Jesus. In fact, the Holy Spirit was given the role of "indwelling" each believer as guide, counselor, convictor, bridge, and comforter. Again, the Holy Spirit worked behind the scenes, so to speak, but was definitely equal in stature and power with God the Father and God the Son. Connor aptly characterizes the uniqueness of the Spirit's role:

> The term Spirit of God is constantly occurring in the Bible. The Spirit of God is distinguishable from God, yet is nothing apart from God. In general, the Spirit of God stands for the energy or power of God working toward a divinely intended event. In the Old Testament the Spirit of God worked in various ways in nature and came upon man to produce various results. In the New Testament this divine presence becomes more distinctly moral in purpose and intimate in nature.

HOLY SPIRIT in the OLD TESTAMENT

The first mention of the Holy Spirit occurs quite early in scripture. Genesis 1:2 records the Spirit's activity in the greater creation story. Being described as God's Spirit solidifies the stance that God the Father and the Holy Spirit are equal entities. This citation in Genesis also confirms the pre-existence of the Holy Spirit as being before creation or any known thing.

The primary functions of the Spirit in the Old Testament are demonstrably different from those recorded in the New Testament. In Hebrew history the Spirit worked on a more corporate level with Israel in contrast to the individual attention found in the New Testament narratives. Of course, this was God's primary approach with the Hebrews as well, seeing them as a Holy Nation and a Nation of Priests. As Eichrodt points out, the "Spirit was the power behind the people of God in Old Testament times."

While no action of the Holy Spirit as recorded in the Old Testament narratives rivals that of Pentecost, the Spirit was at work in many potent ways. Joshua was empowered by the Spirit with leadership skills and wisdom (Num. 27:18); the Judges were empowered to deliver Israel from oppression; when David was anointed King, "the Spirit of the Lord came mightily upon him from that day forward" (1 Sam. 16:13); the Spirit was active in much of the Exodus experience; the Spirit led Saul to ecstatic speech after his anointing (1 Sam. 10:6-11); and the Spirit was predicted to anoint a Servant-Messiah, a deliverer coming in power: "and the Spirit of the Lord shall rest upon him, the spirit of wisdom and understanding, the spirit of counsel and might, the spirit of knowledge and the fear of the Lord. And his delight shall be in the fear of the Lord" (Is. 11:2-3).

HOLY SPIRIT in the NEW TESTAMENT

The work of the Holy Spirit is more open, more vivid and much easier to identify in the New Testament writings. The Spirit was integral in the birth of John the Baptist, born to previously barren

Elizabeth, and "filled with the Holy Spirit even from birth" (Lk. 1:15). The Spirit was deeply active in the virginal conception and birth of Jesus. This is evidenced by the statement the angel made to young Mary: "The Holy Spirit will come upon you, and the power of the Most High will overshadow you. So the holy one to be born will be called the Son of God" (Lk. 1:35). The Spirit was also active in the baptism of Jesus (Mk. 3:13-17), in this case as the descending dove. The baptism event is seen as a spiritual coronation, sanctioned by God the Father and empowered by the Holy Spirit. The Spirit was with Jesus during the temptation episode against Satan and in each miracle performed during his earthly ministry.

Perhaps the most vibrant act of the Holy Spirit came at Pentecost. Pentecost was the culmination of the Hebrew "Feast of Weeks," occurring on the fiftieth day after Passover. As recorded in the synoptic gospels, the Pentecost following the death, resurrection, and ascension of Jesus signaled the dramatic outpouring of the Spirit, and with it the beginning of the Church Age. As people assembled from the many regions, the Spirit empowered the disciples to preach and teach in various languages, or to be heard in all assembled languages. The result was newly empowered disciples and 3000 new converts to faith in the Messiah Christ. Following Pentecost, the Spirit was active in leading the disciples as they preached and founded churches, providing power, wisdom, counsel, and guidance for each new convert and new church.

The New Testament also portrays a ministry of involvement and attention on a distinctly individual level by the Holy Spirit. The Old Testament points primarily to the corporate work of the Spirit while the New Testament sees the Spirit working deeply within each believer. Grudem sees the work of the Spirit as, "giving life, empowering for individual service, purifying, revealing, guiding, directing, providing assurance, teaching, illuminating, and unifying." Garrett adds, "The Spirit convicts as to sin, righteousness and judgment; is at work in prayer, in resistance to sin, and in instruction; aids in the reception and possession of spiritual gifts; and empowers for witnessing."

The Holy Spirit is seen as working intimately with each believer in the role of paraclete. Paraclete is defined as, "one who comes to another's aid...and one who is called to another's side to take his or her part, as a friend, a counselor, always lending aid, a partaker in another's cause" (Oden). The Holy Spirit became the paraclete after the ascension of Jesus, a promise Jesus made as recorded in John 14:16. This level of activity further solidifies the oneness and equality of the Holy Spirit with God the Father and God the Son. Brown puts it this way, "As 'another Paraclete,' the Paraclete is, as it were, another Jesus."

The Greeks compared the Spirit to the breathing forth of an outer breath, the Latins to the breathing forth of an inner love

Bonaventure

TRINITY

To contemplate the Trinity is to entertain perhaps the most complicated concept of all theological study. Scripture doesn't precisely deal with the Trinity in any one section, which enhances the need to cover the whole of scripture in order to create an acceptable definition and concept. With a systematic study of scripture (both Old and New Testaments), one can come to a surprisingly easy understanding of this greatly ethereal concept. This is not to say it will be easy to fathom how God actually exists, or from whence God came. It will simply be easier to understand the ways in which God chooses to reveal... well... reveal God.

To better understand the concept of God as the Trinity, one must move away from the idea that God is a grandfatherly figure dressed in white, sitting on a big chair in heaven. The concept of God as the Trinity is the concept of God as one entity that simultaneously exists in three distinct "persons." Grudem explains it more succinctly:

The word Trinity is never found in the Bible, though the idea represented by the word is taught in many places. The word Trinity means *tri-unity* or *three-in-oneness*. The teaching of scripture is summarized in three statements:

1. God is three persons

2. Each person is fully God

3. There is one God

Baker's Dictionary of the Bible defines the Trinity as, "a convenient designation for the one God self-revealed in Scripture as Father, Son and Holy Spirit. It signifies that within the one essence of the Godhead we have to distinguish three 'persons' who are neither three gods on the one side, nor three parts or modes on the other, but coequally and coeternally God."

Closely tied to the attribution of coequal and coeternal are the concepts of inseparable yet distinguishable. "Only within the triune premise can numerous vexations, perplexities, and errors be resolved. Whatever is said of God is rightly said of Son and Spirit" (Oden). So we have a definition of God as existing in the persons of the Father, Son and Holy Spirit; as one in essence yet distinguishable as three persons; and, as coequal and coeternal. See how easy that was?

Understanding the concept of God as the Trinity becomes even easier when the above view is contrasted with the two competing, yet flawed, concepts. The first and foremost flawed view is called "modalism." Modalism states that the self-revelation and work of the one and only God took place in different ways at different times. In essence, there is one God who fulfills different roles or modes as needed in history. This view was birthed very early in church history by philosophers such as Noetus and Praxeus. Noetus taught that the Father actually submitted to birth, became the Son, and then suffered and died. Sabellius, a student of the early philosophers and a hard line modalist, referred to God as the "Son-Father." He was fully excommunicated by the Roman Church after becoming outspoken as a modalist.

The main problem with modalism as a concept is how hard it is to square with scripture. A case in point, to whom was Jesus praying while in the Garden of Gethsemane before his arrest? A modalist would say that God was filling the role of the Son. If that is correct, then Jesus was merely praying to himself while in the Garden of Gethsemane as he awaited arrest. Another example was Jesus praying aloud while on the cross. Yet another occurred during the baptism of Jesus as God spoke from above. Would a self-respecting modalist be forced to admit that no one was actually home in heaven and Jesus was merely praying to himself? Even worse, was Jesus practicing ventriloquism during his baptism? These examples and subsequent questions are why modalism is so easy to disqualify.

Another flawed theological view is called tritheism. This view sees the three persons of the Godhead as three distinctly different Gods. Tritheism essentially views the Father, the Son and the Holy Spirit as separate Gods who work together to accomplish each other's purposes. It takes a village to do many things in life, but certainly not to define God.

Once more, the best theological view of the Trinity is to see God as three persons who make up one essence. There is a unity of essence, of purpose and of endeavor within the three persons of the Godhead.

> ...All (Father, Son and Holy Spirit) are One, by unity of substance; while the mystery of the dispensation is still guarded, which distributes the Unity into a Trinity, placing in their order the three Persons, the Father, the Son and the Holy Ghost: three, however, not in condition, but in form; not in power, but in aspect; yet of one substance, and of one condition, and of one power, inasmuch as he is the one God (Tertullian).

Thus the Trinity is best defined as One God made up of three Persons, who are linked in essence and by unity of purpose and endeavor.

Holy, holy, holy, Lord God almighty,
Holy, holy, holy, merciful and mighty;
God in three persons, blessed Trinity.

SIN

It seems the majority of humankind's history could be summed up with the word "rebellion." Soon after creation, people were in perfect union with God. Early Genesis tells the story of God and humankind existing (literally) together in a unique paradise. This was God's intended plan through creation. Of course, a facet of God's plan was also to give his created people a choice in the matter. So what are the odds that the first people would have made a really bad choice and screwed up paradise? Quite high, it seems, since they basically did just that. This is the first example of humankind's rebellion against God's plans and purposes...but certainly not the last.

Simply put, this rebellion against God is called sin. Not much of a word really, just three letters, but these three letters have shaped the destiny of all people. Sin, the rebellion against all God is and all God stands for, is a life condition that one battles for the full ride. It is a reality of birth to enter into a world permeated with evil and wrong. Augustine called this joint condition an effect of the "original sin." It's not so much that the first sin actually affected the DNA of all to follow. Better understood, it affected the existence into which all people are born. The effects of sin and rebellion are everywhere to be found, both inside and outside each individual. There is but one remedy available for our sin condition and that is God's salvation. But salvation is a time-release cure that won't take full effect until the next life. Until that point, sin is an enemy to be faced each day. Salvation takes away much of the penalty of sin, but none of its presence.

SIN DEFINED

"Sin is the failure to conform to the moral law of God in act, attitude and nature" (Grudem). Sin consists not only of acts, such as lying, stealing, etc., but also in attitudes that are contrary to God's plans for us. Very simply put, God provides parameters within which we are to live. The parameters are for both thoughts and actions, and are clearly defined by scripture. All existence outside these parameters is sin.

> By sin, he understands, not only sinful acts, such as theft, lying and murder, but also a state in which man finds himself, and which is expressed in self-esteem, self-coronation, and rebellion against God (Taylor).

> Sin is man's turning away from God and toward himself in order that he might make himself the center and focus of all reality (McKelway).

Sin can also be defined as estrangement from God. The thought here is much like a unilateral separation brought on by one party in a relationship. This estrangement (sin condition) is firmly in place before salvation is acted upon, and can return at any point afterward due to a person's acts and thoughts. "Sin is a universal fact before an individual act, or more precisely, sin as an individual act actualizes the universal fact of estrangement" (Tillich).

Much more simply put, all people are born into an estranged relationship with God that can only be rectified (redeemed) through God's provision of salvation. However, even believers can allow estrangement to merge back into their lives at points in time after salvation begins. This is done through acts of sin and by dereliction of ones relationship with God. The sad reality exists that sin, as a state, and as acts of choice, can separate a person from God.

SIN versus SINS

This "estranged" position of being outside of God's plans and purposes can be seen simply as sin. Thus, there is a huge difference between sin and sins. Sin is a condition of being human and of being naturally outside of God's salvation. Sins are the outcomes, byproducts or results of the sin condition. Only one of the aforementioned states can be remedied. One will always be human (while alive) and thus, subject to all of the issues related to that condition. However, one can "come in from the cold," so-to-speak, and be brought to God through salvation.

> Contrary to the legal model, sin is not simply a set of behaviors to
> be avoided. Much more fundamentally, it is a way of life to be
> exposed and changed, and no one is innocent (Taylor).

Barbara Brown Taylor adds, "The choice to enter into a process of repair is called repentance, an often bitter medicine with the undisputed power to save lives."

This state of sin we are born into will never fully leave us, even after salvation is accepted and acted upon. Sin is the state of life when we are distanced from God. We are born into this unfortunate condition and can return to it even after we become Christians. All acts or thoughts that occur at any point in life are sins. We must not confuse the two. Some think, "sin, sins, what's the difference? No big deal!" It is a very big deal indeed. We are talking about the difference between "doing wrong" and "being wrong." The actual difference is staggering. If the "being" part is attended to, then the "doing" part will occur less often and will be less damaging. Again, sin is the state of being separated from God. Sins are but the byproducts of our distance from God.

SIN as SEPARATION

We've established that sin is a condition or state of distance from God. This condition is a natural one, one into which all people are born. This "existential" condition (or one having to do with basic existence) is the foremost sin problem faced by humankind. But it isn't a condition that we can control. As hard as one may try, the sin condition will never be done away with in this life. There is a facet of sin, however, that a person can influence and even control. The reality of choosing to sin is one most people do not enjoy dealing with. It's much more fun to cite the vagaries of being chained to a "birth effect" of inherited sin. Who wants to evaluate the amount of negative activities present in daily living? The Hebrews did exactly that through day-to-day living (they saw a direct correlation between righteousness and how one lived) and through the ways they defined sin. In fact, we still employ age-old definitions of sin created by the Hebrews.

Sin as Missing the Mark: Seen as missing a target with a bow and arrow and as going astray. This is not necessarily to sin intentionally, although it could be; it is more veering off the course purposed by God.

Sin as an Act of Wrong: This is seen as a volitional, intentional and deliberate choice to go against God's purposes and parameters. This is when one follows through on an act or thought, even though they know it is the wrong thing to do.

Sin as Rebellion: This is more than an intentional wrong, it is full scale rebellion against God.

Both sin as a condition and sins that result from that condition can be seen as separation from God. Those who have not yet accepted God's personal salvation are existentially separated. The redeemed who have accepted salvation yet engage in serial and habitual sin, or those who do not regularly confess sin and seek restoration, are also separated from God. The former state of separation is a no-fault one, while the latter is squarely the fault and result of personal decisions.

Bottom Line: The possibility of being distanced from God is apparent throughout life. Once salvation is accepted and the existential separation is alleviated, one must focus on not allowing the separation to reappear. If the distance is once again spanned, it is plainly the fault of the believer.

UNPARDONABLE SIN

Much angst has arisen over the issue of the unpardonable sin. "Could I have committed this transgression and now be doomed to Hell?" Many people have asked a similar question at some point or another, genuinely worried about their future. Thankfully, if the question is genuine and the fear is real, then the answer is "No." So, why do people worry about such a far-fetched possibility of losing salvation over the commission of one sin? What could be so bad that it would nullify God's provision of salvation? The main reason people actually worry about sinning to the point of doom is simply bad theology. Poor interpretations of scripture or skipping scripture and merely going with traditional hear-say are the biggest culprits here.

Over the years there have been many sins or acts cited as being the unpardonable sin. Many believe that this sin is ignoring God throughout life and thus dying without salvation. No doubt scripture is clear that an eternity without God awaits all who do not opt for salvation; but is this really the unpardonable sin? No, not by a long shot, and the reason why is simple: how could someone commit a sin without pardon when they haven't yet received any pardon whatsoever through salvation? Another idea promoted is that suicide is the unpardonable sin. Directly on the philosophical heels of suicide is the notion that murder is a sin without pardon. Is either correct? Neither opinion is backed up by scripture, so neither is to be seen as the sin of all sins. Others cite using God's name in vain, especially by cursing, as the sin of doom. Bad taste yes, but certainly not the unpardonable sin.

Scripture is actually quite clear on the sin without pardon. It is cited in Matthew 12: 31-32, "Therefore I tell you, every sin and blasphemy will be forgiven men, but the blasphemy against the Spirit will not be forgiven. And whoever says a word against the Son of Man will be forgiven; but whoever speaks against the Holy Spirit will not be forgiven, either in this age or in the age to come." Mark 3:29-30 also focuses on this unique blasphemy as Jesus says, "Whoever blasphemes against the Holy Spirit never has forgiveness."

These verses obviously have nothing to do with cursing, suicide or murder. The actual intent was pointed to those who had literally slandered the name and work of the Holy Spirit. Grudem explains it as: "unusually malicious, willful rejection and slander against the Holy Spirit's work attesting to Christ, and attributing that work to Satan." The Pharisees' forceful rejection of Christ's authenticity led to this dire warning (Matthew 12:24). Out of spiritual blindness and personal arrogance, they attributed the various miracles of Christ to the power of Satan.

So relax. It would be hard for a self-respecting Christian to commit the "real" unpardonable sin.

Sin: the power of an unholy choice

SALVATION

"What was the ultimate cause that led to Christ's coming to earth and dying for our sins?" (Grudem). The answer is salvation, but that's the easiest part of this equation. Salvation is a complex and involved concept that has wide-reaching implications. Plus, salvation is an inclusive term that easily spawns multiple words that are integral to the overall concept. Simply put, there isn't one term that adequately defines salvation. Then there's the "sticking" issue of salvation, or whether or not one's salvation is secure and everlasting. Suffice it to say that salvation is much more than simply being "saved," but it does begin there...and so will we.

SAVED

It's quite common for someone who accepts Christ's offer of salvation to be deemed saved. "I was saved at a revival last week," or "I got saved at Vacation Bible School when I was 10." The pressing question is "Saved from what?" Normally people are saved from obvious things such as burning buildings or raging water. So what exactly are people saved from when they accept God's salvation?

In the previous chapter, we dealt with the natural sin condition that creates distance from God. The only remedy from the complete hold of this natural sin condition is salvation. So, in effect, one is saved from that innate condition. The sin condition comes with an automatic penalty of spiritual death. It also creates a great deal of on-going negative power within an individual. Salvation remedies both these ills, saving one from the penalty and power of the natural sin condition.

With other biblical concepts like deliverance and liberation, the word salvation evokes the rescue of persons caught in a hopeless situation. The image suggests that we were all held prisoners by the evil one in the strongholds of death when Christ, through his own death, overcame the enemy, saved us from his power, and set us free. Since God desires everyone to be saved and to come to the knowledge of the truth, Jesus Christ, the one mediator between God and humankind, came into the world to save us (1 Tim. 1:15; 2:4-5)" (Bilezikian).

Salvation has had all sorts of meanings in the course of its journeys around the by-ways of the history of doctrine — people have thought of salvation as rescue and restoration, as revelation and reconciliation, as representation and substitution, as judgment and making righteous, as incarnation and atonement, as decontamination from the things of this world, and as attainment of a heavenly realm — accompanied by prosperity, liberation and justice (Newlands).

SALVATION as ATONEMENT

Atonement is the facet of salvation that focuses on the sin payment and sacrifice of Jesus. The idea is that some rendering or satisfaction must be offered for wrong-doing. For believers, the once-for-all sacrifice of Jesus was offered to offset the penalty of our sin condition. Hobbs calls it "at-one-ment" and sees it as "covering one's sin penalty." Think of it as having a really large debt that is suddenly paid in full by someone else. There remains no cost to you at all; all portions of the debt have been retired and forgiven. This is also the portion of salvation known as "grace."

God's purposes of redemption and reconciliation are accomplished in the death and resurrection of Jesus. The fulfillment of these purposes will only be achieved when all things are brought into their unity in Christ. Thus, the cross becomes a symbol of divine intent, a display of God's loving purposes. The cross is the instrument of salvation. Christ crucified is the wisdom and power of God. It is through the death and resurrection that God acts to heal, to reconcile and to make whole (Moses).

SALVATION as JUSTIFICATION

Justification is the most legal of terms associated with salvation. Biblically speaking, to be justified is to be given a verdict of "not guilty." Just as with atonement, a penalty was necessary due to the pervasive sin condition known to all people. By Jesus' death, a justification was provided to all people (upon their acceptance) that effectively canceled out their individual penalty. John Murray writes, "Justification is primarily that judgment against the individual has been canceled. This is a pardon."

Among New Testament writers, Paul is the undisputed champion of justification, but not for the reasons one might assume. His tendency was to promote justification, but mostly as a guard against a "works-based" theology of saving faith. Roman and Greek religious practice was extremely performance oriented. Much the same could be said for orthodox Hebrew beliefs and practices. The Old Testament required the Hebrews to observe certain Holy Days and ritual periods, and to provide regular sacrifices to atone for sin. It was not uncommon for new converts, regardless of their backgrounds, to bring into their new faith many of these performance-based ideas of atonement. For the integrity of the new faith, Paul promoted works as useless for salvation. To Paul, salvation was entirely based on God's grace and had nothing to do with the merit of humankind. This, in a nutshell, is a proper definition of justification.

SALVATION as SANCTIFICATION

Thus far, all aspects of salvation have been acts of God on behalf of his created people. Sanctification is the first part of the salvation equation in which the individual becomes a somewhat equal player. Of course, God remains central to the process, but in sanctification each believer shares responsibility for the progress of salvation. Garrett states, "What the righteousness of God is to justification, the holiness of God is to sanctification." So, sanctification is that part of salvation where each person begins to move toward holiness.

The Old Testament idea of sanctification was to be "holy and clean." In Leviticus, God states, "...be holy because I am holy." This means that the individual believer is charged with the responsibility of seeking to grow spiritually, with the goal being the holiness of God. The New Testament adds Christ-likeness to the model and, in effect, raises the bar on the expected pursuit of personal holiness.

G. Abbot Smith sees sanctification as, "Being set apart for moral goodness. To be set apart designates not merely the fact that believers are formally set apart, or belong to Christ, but that they are then to conduct themselves accordingly. They are to live lives of purity and goodness." One theologian refers to the process of sanctification as "moral renovation." Simply put, it is the personal spiritual growth process whereby a believer progressively moves in the direction of Christ's example.

SALVATION as a PROCESS

It is quite easy to view salvation as an event that happens at one moment in time. This once-for-all view of salvation is truly unbalanced and will lead to gross dysfunction at some point. Salvation actually has many elements and is inherently progressive in nature. Perhaps salvation can best be appreciated when understood in terms of phases. Simply described, one is saved, one is being saved, and one will be saved. Despite the fact that preachers often urge "sinners" to come forward and be "saved," salvation is much more involved. The initial point of salvation is but the beginning of a life-long process. Think of the initial point of salvation (accepting or "getting saved") as a transaction. As a process that follows, however, salvation never ends.

I AM SAVED: the process begins with an act

I AM BEING SAVED: growing and the process of salvation

I WILL BE SAVED: eternal existence with God

Is salvation to be understood as something which has happened to the believer? Or is it something currently happening? Or is there there an eschatological dimension to it — in other words, is there something which has yet to happen? (McGrath).

The answers to those questions are yes, yes and yes! Salvation begins as an act of belief and acceptance and is to be progressively in effect for (literally) eternity.

ONCE SAVED ALWAYS SAVED

The eternal security of salvation has long been a hot topic in theology. Obviously there is no middle ground on this issue. Salvation is either rock solid secure or it is not. As exists with most theological topics, there are two main schools of thought on this subject. One view sees salvation as fully secure due to Christ's once-for-all act on the cross. Paul's statements in Romans 8: 38-39 are often used to support the eternal security stance. The other view cites the overall fickleness of people and the built-in proclivity to sin as rationale for salvation being tenuous. In this alternate view, God is trustworthy to provide for salvation, but people are inconsistent in faithing God in return. Hebrews 6:6 and 10:39 are used to support this side of the argument.

To say that salvation, after being embraced, can never be lost, is a very positive and comforting statement. Obviously it's not called eternal security for nothing! However, questions do arise regarding those who faith and trust God at one point in life but who later move away from their faith. Would a lapse in faith also create a lapse of salvation? Is it possible to veer off faith's track to the point of losing one's salvation? And if so, exactly how far afield does a person have to veer before the loss of salvation occurs? These questions illustrate the extremely slippery slope that is the study of salvation's security. It is one thing to cite salvation as being non-secure but quite another to pick out the exact point that salvation is nullified. Unfortunately, scripture isn't of supreme help in this debate either.

By selecting certain texts in the New Testament, a case could easily be made for either view.

Yet, the eternal security of salvation is a foundational Baptist doctrine. This said, it must be added that many other major Protestant groups deny the security of salvation. So who's right? What's the correct answer? Isn't there a great deal on the line here?

Bottom Line: This issue is not definitively covered in scripture, so there are only interpretations available. Since there really is no absolute right or wrong stance, each person must decide for themselves what they believe about this issue. Rather than debate the validity of either view, why not hope Baptists are right, but just in case, live as if they are wrong! There may be a middle ground after all.

...evil made totally explicit is resolved in the forgiveness of God.
Gratia gratis data (grace which is freely given)

HEAVEN

*Thou hast made us for thyself, and therefore our hearts
are restless until they rest in thee*

The words of Augustine will probably register truest when taking the long view of life. On a very good day, do we actually long for heaven? After all, it takes dying to get there, right? It seems most people are content living this life, and they would rather wait for the next phase to materialize. This seems to be true even for the redeemed believer who sees heaven as his or her eternal home. Ever wonder why people feel, as the country-western song states, "I want to go to heaven. I just don't wanna' go tonight"? Is it that most people don't know what to expect, so they are not in a hurry to arrive? Or, could it be that life as we know it today isn't that bad and most people are quite satisfied with their lives? It might be a tie, especially since early twenty-first-century living is at a record best in the West. So, let's take the tack of explaining heaven in simple and understandable ways so it won't remain a familiar, yet foreign, topic.

C. S. Lewis sees death as a "severe mercy," meaning heaven will be exponentially better than the lives we presently lead. But, what will it be like? Will heaven be one (very) long church service? Will it be an eternal learning process? Are the streets really made of gold? Is white *de rigeur*? Will people recognize each other, and if so, what age will people appear in eternity? These are now age-old questions that, for the most part, cannot be answered by simply studying scripture. Scripture is remarkably nonspecific about the particulars of heaven, and most often utilizes symbolism to paint simple pictures. However, scripture is all we have as a basis for theological study, so, it is from scripture that we will frame our study.

HEAVEN is a PROMISED REALITY

Heaven is consistently promised in the New Testament as the place for the redeemed to spend eternity in God's presence. John 14:2 reads, "In my Father's house are many dwelling places; if it were not so I would have told you; for I go to prepare a place for you." Acts 7:55-56 records the final experience of Stephen the Martyr: "But Stephen was full of the Holy Spirit. He looked up to Heaven and saw the glory of God and Jesus standing at God's right side. He said, 'Look! I see Heaven open and the Son of Man standing at God's right side.'" These verses prove that heaven is a reality that is consistently promised in scripture. "No eye has seen, no ear has heard, no mind has conceived what God has promised for those who love him" (1 Cor. 2:9).

HEAVEN BRINGS NEWNESS

A verse in Revelation chapter 21 reads, "Look, I am making all things new!" The Greek word for *new* used in this verse has a unique meaning. New is normally defined in a chronological sense, such as new clothes or a new opportunity. The descriptive word "fresh" also comes to mind when this version of new is utilized. In contrast, the word translated *new* in Revelation means a *qualitative newness*, something heretofore unknown, unprecedented, and unique. This suggests that heaven will be an unprecedented existence, one that is completely indescribable. It isn't a surprise to hear that heaven will be unprecedented; this isn't news at all. The value here is that due to the unique qualitative newness of heaven, all descriptions are simply best attempts to paint a magnificent picture.

Despite the fact that scripture describes heaven as having walls of jasper and streets of gold, it most likely won't showcase either. New Testament writers utilized examples found in an emperor's palace in describing heaven. Why? A magnificent palace was a grand, yet understandable example that all people could relate to. For the common person, the palace examples/descriptions would be heavenly indeed. Heaven is also described metaphorically, written in the language of earthly delight (sound, sight, taste, smell and touch). This approach provides for Christians a truly personal connection between this life and the one to follow. So, view heaven as being qualitatively unparalled to any and all previous thoughts or experiences, and then expect it to be exponentially better!

THE LOCATION of HEAVEN

Ask just about anyone where heaven is located, and they will point up. Why? Well it's a known fact that hell is down and heaven is up, right? Best bet would be to rotate and point in every possible direction and then to admit that no one holds a clue as to the actual location of heaven. Scripture never attempts to provide precise information about anything other than heaven's reality.

Jesus never provides information on where Heaven is located — by implication and direct statement he demonstrates that it is a domain of God — in effect, "Heaven is where God is" (Gutherie).

Many heavens are spoken of in the New Testament, as the term is also used to describe the near and far away skies, stars and galaxies. Best bet is to view the location of heaven as existing in a different dimension, just as God exists outside of our created dimension. For this reason, the location of heaven was not provided. Heaven is a place we should strive to go, not a location we should strive to know!

WHAT WILL WE LOOK LIKE?

Who hasn't pondered such a question at some point in their faith journey? We will be different, that's for sure, but exactly what we will look like is not clear. 1 Corinthians 15:42-49 describes theheavenly form as a spiritual body that does not decay, is spirit powered, cannot be destroyed and will be perfect. Philippians 3:21 states, "By his power to rule all things, he will change our simple bodies and make them like his own glorious body."

The best interpretation is that our bodies will be supernatural, in all facets. Jesus, post-resurrection, is an example of what the spiritual body will be like. He was recognizable, he ate, held conversations, went through walls and doors. So, will we be like that? This is hard to know, since we can't minimize the fact that Jesus continued his ministry-mission after his resurrection. Scripture does state that all traces of humanity will fade and the spiritual body will reflect the supernatural existence. Thus, no pain, disease or other psycho-physical infirmities will be present. It's clear that all vestiges of human frailty will be abolished, and the result will be perfection.

The question, "will we know each other in heaven?" is possibly the most asked of all related inquiries. Most theologians believe that those known in this life will also be known in heaven (if not, name tags will be helpful there as well). New Testament sections seen as supporting this belief are Matthew 8:11 and Matthew 22:31-32, as well as the transfiguration event. Jeffrey Burton Russell sees this issue in another frame with a focus on the retention of individuality in the afterlife: "The salvation of the community does not mean that the individual is submerged. Rather, one joins with God and with others in the "ecclesia" (church/faith) in the communion of the saints without losing one's identity. Individuality remains as an incandescence amidst the great glow of light."

REWARDS

Another commonly held belief is that rewards will be provided in heaven for outstanding faith achievements in this life. Actually, scripture is inconsistent on this subject, which shouldn't be surprising at this point of our study. Most sections cited as supporting rewards are found in the parables, which are teaching stoies. One in particular is the parable of the three servants in Luke, which states, "I will let you rule over ten cities." Is this a promise of heavenly rewards? Some theologians say yes, while others say no. Mark records these words, "I tell you the truth, whoever gives you a drink of water because you belong to the Christ will truly get his reward." Is this reward one to be received in the afterlife, or is this simply a spiritual blessing? In all honesty, no one knows the answers to the rewards questions. The middle ground was taken by Bloesch:

> We are accepted into heaven on the basis of faith alone, but we are adorned in heaven on the basis of the fruits of our faith. I do not perceive levels in heaven...,but I contend...that there will be distinctions in heaven, though no unlawful discriminations.

In summary, heaven is a genuine existence promised by Jesus as recorded in scripture. The particulars of exactly what heaven will be like, or how one will appear, are quite sketchy. However, those issues should be subordinate to the present faith life and to the promise of being with God for eternity.

> Heaven itself cannot be described, but the human concept of heaven can be. Heaven is not dull; it is not static; it is not monochrome. It is an endless dynamic of joy in which one is ever more oneself as one was meant to be, in which one increasingly realizes one's potential in understanding as well as love and is filled more and more with wisdom. It is to be the discovery of one's deepest self...For Christians, heaven is where Christ is. Going to heaven, or better, being in heaven, is being in the presence of Christ (Russell).

modicum et vos videbitis me
(yet a little while and you shall see me)

HELL

Hell is the "other" eternal destination depicted in scripture. Once again, however, scripture is quite inconsistent in its statements concerning hell. Suffice it to say, scripture is clear on the reality of hell, but not as much so as to the duration and content of the negative afterlife. Jesus likened hell to an actual valley outside of Jerusalem widely used as a garbage dump. Earlier in Hebrew history the Valley of Hinnom was the site of child sacrifice to the pagan god Molech (2 Kings 23). It had been relegated to a dump for garbage, waste materials and dead animals by the early first century. As Jesus used the area to describe the afterlife for unbelievers, people could see fires smoldering and smell the putrid odors of burning, decaying flesh. They were familiar with sounds of wild dogs howling and gnashing their teeth as they fought over garbage. Needless to say, the listeners perceived the intended picture of a place to avoid. Translated into Greek, this Hebrew place becomes *gehenna*. Jesus used *gehenna* eleven times to describe hell.

> Gehenna is the Greek form of the Aramic name for a valley south of Jerusalem. This valley saw child sacrifice and other affronts to Hebrew faith; as well as a place of criminal execution. Thus, Gehenna became a metaphor for shame, unrighteousness and suffering (Hanson).

The word *sheol* was also used numerous times to describe the afterlife. Sheol is mainly an Old Testament-Hebrew view of a place for the dead, both the good and bad, righteousness and unrighteous. *Sheol* literally means "unknown," and when combined with its Greek equivalent, *Hades*, it is seen as meaning "unseen world." "Sheol was regarded as an underground region (Num. 16:30; Amos

9:2), shadowy and gloomy, where disembodied souls had a conscious but dull and inactive existence (2 Sam. 22:6; Eccl. 9:10). The Hebrew people regarded Sheol as a place to which the righteous and unrighteous go at death (Gen. 37:35; Ps. 9:17; Is. 38:10), a place where punishment is received and rewards are enjoyed. However, God is present in Sheol (Ps. 139:8). It is open and known to him (Job 26:6; Prov. 15:11). This suggests that in death God's people remain under his care, and the wicked never escape his judgment" (Lockyer).

Sheol was such an entrenched Hebrew belief that it is truly amazing to see the concept of the afterlife shift so dramatically as it did in the New Testament. Mainly the New Testament writers viewed hell as either Gehenna or Hades, and saw a distinction between the eternal place for the righteous and the unrighteous.

There are 162 references to hell in the New Testament, with Jesus speaking on the subject as much as any other. Hell was also a hot (sorry) topic with Matthew, with the bulk of New Testament references found in his letter. Matthew mostly refers to the conditions of hell, citing it as hot (13:43; 25:41) and dark (8:12; 22:13; 25:30). Theology's biggest concern regarding hell has always been the *literal* question. Are the references to hell found in the New Testament to be taken literally?

> There are a number of New Testament images for hell: it is described as a place of unquenchable and eternal fire, a place of outer darkness where there is weeping and gnashing of teeth, a place where the undying worm torments hell's inhabitants. It is the lake of fire and brimstone, the second death. It is a place of destruction where the inhabitant is forever cut off from the presence of the Lord. The big question for a person today is, "Are we supposed to take these literally?" (Rumford)

With so many disparate views on hell having been given credence over time, it isn't any wonder that a great deal of confusion continues to reign. Some see hell as completely metaphorical, while others see it as a literal place complete with sulphur fumes and lapping flames. So who's right? Once again, no one really knows the correct answer. Scripture only gives us information to confirm the reality of hell, but not enough to complete a genuine description of what it is like. Simply put, it is entirely interpretational. Hopefully the following established views will assist in a more thorough understanding of at least the options available for belief:

Britian's Evangelical Alliance identified five positions on hell:
(1) Eternal Conscious Physical and Spiritual Torment
(2) Eternal Conscious Spiritual Torment
(3) Eternal Separation From God
(4) Conditional Immortality
(5) Annihilationism

Flowing from these standard yet disparate views are the following:

Literal View: (1) Hell is a place of punishment that lasts forever. (2) All New Testament descriptions of hell are true and literal. (3) Some in hell will be punished more severely than others (implied in Mark 12:40; Luke 12:47-48). (4) Punishment is physical, mental and emotional. (5) Hell is dark. (6) Hell is infested with worms (Mark 9:44-48).

Metaphorical View: (1) Hell is for the unsaved. (2) Extreme pain and environmental conditions described in the Bible are not to be interpreted literally-these are symbolic. (3) Two primary characteristics of hell are fire and darkness, which conflict since fire would lessen darkness, so they must be symbolic.

Purgatorial View: This view is uniquely Roman Catholic and is roundly dismissed by Protestants. Purgatory is seen as a type of temporary hell where those who die with unconfessed sins not erased through church sacraments will go to be "cleansed." A stay in Purgatory could last years, centuries or even millennia based on the degree of purification necessary. It is believed that after the requisite cleansing an individual will be allowed into heaven.

Conditional View: This view suggests that punishment will take place for a period of time but won't be everlasting. After a process of punishment the individual will be redeemed and restored to a place of blessing.

Annihilationist View: This view is both simple and succinct: the lost will be destroyed or annihilated after life ends. Variations of this view describe a simple slipping away into nothingness and the more dramatic actual destruction of the individual.

When the bible describes hell in terms of death, perishing, destruction or corruption, it suggests that hell marks the end of a wicked person's existence, not its continuation. The language speaks of a cessation of being, not of everlasting existence (Junkins).

Clark Pinnock writes, "Hell is not the beginning of an immortal life in torment but the end of a life of rebellion."

These divergent views prove that there is no such thing as a common concept of hell. Choices abound regarding the nature, length and environment of hell. Theology's biggest problem in dealing with hell is the question of literal interpretation of scripture. Are we to take the descriptions provided in the New Testament to be the actual way hell will look and feel? Or, is it better to look at such descriptions symbolically and see hell as being indescribably bad?

By weighing arguments, position and views on all sides, and citing scripture's historically heavy use of symbolism, it seems appropriate to take a somewhat non-literal view of hell. Scripture is clear on the reality of hell. While symbolism was used by Jesus in portraying the garbage dump outside Jerusalem as hell, it's clear that he was referring to a real place (albeit in another dimension).

It seems apparent that the New Testament writers were taking the same tack in describing hell as was taken in describing heaven. The allusions to fire, smell, pain and the like were likely the most vivid examples at hand to describe a "place without God." The same would go for "darkness and gnashing teeth," both symbols of a bad existence in a very bad place. The descriptions of fire and pervasive darkness also lend credence to the non-literal approach. Jude describes hell as "eternal fire" in verse 7, and then later depicts it as the "blackest darkness" in verse 13. The best approach in understanding hell is to see it as a place of total and complete separation from God and all things of God. Imagine the most wicked and vile existence possible, and then multiply that many times over. Hell will be an existence without God!

> Do not try to imagine what it is like to be in hell, the mistake is to take such pictures as physical descriptions, when in fact they are imagery symbolizing realities far worse than the symbols themselves (Packer).

> All the words for Hell, Gehenna, Sheol and Hades all indicate separation from God. If God's overarching plan for creation was for fellowship — then the extreme opposite would be separation (Hanson).

> What (C.S.) Lewis is talking about is the pain of missing heaven, or in the language of medieval scholastics, *poena damni*. This kind of torment comes not from active punishment inflicted by God-like flames scorching the skin — but from having no contact with the One who is the source of peace (Crockett).

abandon all hope, you who enter

Epilogue

Hopefully it's apparent that theology doesn't have to be either hard, difficult or deep. Theology is simply thinking about God in reference to faith and life. Theology is also about faithing a God that can't be seen or heard. God can, however, be felt. In the inner-most portion of our created being exists a soul. This soul is but a void, until it is made complete through our acceptance of God's act of salvation. From that point forward, the soul becomes the point of faith-contact with a loving, caring, just and merciful God. Along the way can come growth and progress in faith that will, in time, achieve the purposes of God for this life. Along faith's way, one will come to a deeper understanding of Jesus, the Holy Spirit, God as Trinity, sin and sins, salvation, heaven and hell, and of course, scripture. The goal of this life in faith is to become more complete in all ways, with one of them being understanding. This is theology pure and simple. It is the process of attending to our faith and growing in the understanding of what it means to be a believer in the Most High God. It is also a privilege!

To paraphrase the Great Commission as found in Matthew 28:

"Therefore go forth and be theologians!"

Is it fair to say I was lured away by endless distractions and lovelier attractions, or fairer still, my own free will is the better one to blame for this familiar mess I've made again. So I would understand if You were out of patience, and I would understand if I was out of chances. I would understand if You would make me pay, I would understand lying in the bed I made again. Let me sing a new song, old things are gone! Everyday it's true, You make all Your mercies new!

Nordeman, Peacock & Norman

CITATIONS

Aquinas, Thomas *Summa Contra Gentiles*, II.

Augustine *de doctrina Christiana*, II.

Augustine *de utiliate credendi*, III.

Augustine *Confessions*, trans. Henry Chadwick (Oxford: Clarebdon Press, 1991).

Baker's Dictionary of Theology, Everett F. Harrison, Gen. Ed. 1960.

Barclay, William *Jesus As They Saw Him* (Grand Rapids: Eerdmans, 1962).

Barth, Karl *Church Dogmatics*, 14 vols. (Edinburgh: Clark, 1936-75).

Berkhof, Hendrikus *Christian Faith* (Grand Rapids: Eerdmans, 1979).

Bloesch, Donald *Holy Scripture: Revelation, Inspiration, & Interpretation* (Downers Grove: IVP, 1994).

Bonaventure, *In IV Sent*, preface in *Opera Theologica selecta*.

Comfort, P. W. Gen. Ed. *The Origin of the Bible* (Wheaton Il.: Tyndale, 1992).

Connor, W. T. *Christian Doctrine* (Nashville: Broadman, 1960).

Crockett, William Gen. Ed. *Four Views on Hell* (Grand Rapids: Zondervan, 1996).

Eichrodt, W. *Theology of the New Testament* TDNT VII, (Semeion, 1961).

Evans, C. Stephen *The Quest For Faith* (Downers Grove: IVP, 1986).

Garrett, James Leo *Systematic Theology*, Vols. I-II (Grand Rapids: Eerdmans, 1990 & 1995).

Goppelt, Leonhard *The Typological Interpretation of the Old Testament in the New Testament,* trans. Donald H. Madrig (Grand Rapids: Eerdmans, 1982).

Gore, Charles *Incarnation of the Son of God,* 1981.

Grudem, Wayne *Bible Doctrine* (Grand Rapids: Zondervan, 1999).

Gutherie, Donald *New Testament Theology* (Leicester, UK: IVP, 1981).

Hanson, B. C. *Introduction to Christian Theology* (Minneapolis: Fortress Press, 1977).

Hick, John *The Second Christianity* (London: SCM Press, 1983).

Hobbs, Herschel *Fundamentals of Our Faith* (Nashville: Broadman, 1960).

Horton, W. M. *Christian Theology* (New York: Harper, 1955).

Judkins, E. Anni "Unquenchable Fire," in *Heaven & Hell*, Christian Reflection (Center for Christian Ethics, Waco: Baylor, 2002).

Kendall, R. T. *Understanding Theology* (Ross-Shire, UK: Christian Focus, 1996).

Kreeft, Peter *Heaven: The Heart's Deepest Longing* (San Francisco: Ignatius Press, 1980).

Kreeft, Peter & Ronald Tacelli *Handbook of Christian Apologetics* (Downers Grove: IVP, 1994).

McGrath, Alister *Christian Theology: An Introduction* (Oxford: Blackwell, 2001).

McGrath, Alister *Christian Spirituality* (Oxford: Blackwell, 1999).

McGrath, Alister *Understanding the Trinity* (Eastbourne, UK: Kingsway, 1987).

McGrath, Alister *The Enigma of the Cross* (London: Hodder & Stoughton, 1987).

McKelway, Alex *The Systematic Theology of Paul Tillich* (London: Lutterworth Press, 1964).

Moberly, Walter in *Exploring the Christian Faith* (Nashville: Thomas Nelson:, 1996).

Moses, John *The Sacrifice of God* (Norwich, UK: Canterbury Press, 1992).

Murray, John *Redemption Accomplished & Applied* (Grand Rapids: Eerdmans, 1955).

Newlands, G. M. *The Love of God* (London: Collins, 1980).

Nordeman, Nicole, Charlie Peacock & Bebo Norman Ariose Music, from *Woven and Spun*, the CD.

Oden, Thomas *Systematic Theology, Vols. 1-3* (San Francisco: Harper & Row, 1997, 1989, 1992).

Packer, J. I. *Concise Theology* (Wheaton, IL.: Tyndale House, 1993).

Packer, J. I. *Fundamentalism and the Word of God* (Grand Rapids: Eerdmans, 1958).

Packer, J. I. "The Problem of Eternal Punishment," *Crux* 26 (Sept. 1990).

Payley, William *Works 6* (London: Rivington, 1830).

Pinnock, Clark "The Conditional View," in *Four Views on Hell* (Grand Rapids: Zondervan, 1992).

Rumford, Douglas J. *"What about Heaven & Hell?"* (Wheaton: Tyndale House, 1999).

Russell, Jeffrey B. *A History of Heaven* (Princeton, NJ: Princeton Press, 1997).

Shedd, F. J. *Theology For Beginners* (Ann Arbor MI: Servant Books, 1958).

Spoto, Donald *The Hidden Jesus* (New York: Saint Martins Press, 1999).

Taylor, Vincent *The Cross of Christ* (London: MacMillan, 1956).

Taylor, Barbara Brown *Speaking of Sin* (Boston: Cowley Books, 2000).

Thiessen, H. C. *Introductory Lectures in Systematic Theology* (Grand Rapids: Eerdmans, 1956).

Tillich, Paul *Systematic Theology Vol. III* (Chicago: University of Chicago Press, 1957).

Urban, *Epistle, ANF VIII.*

Whale, J. S. *Christian Doctrine* (Cambridge, UK: Cambridge Press, 1941).

GLOSSARY OF THEOLOGICAL TERMS

Apologetics   The defense of the Christian faith.

Atonement   Literally meaning at-one-ment; a term used to describe the work of Christ in reconciling God and humankind.

Beatitudes   A term for the eight promises of blessing found in the opening section of the Sermon on the Mount (Matthew 5:3-11) "Blessed are the pure…"

Canon   Literally meaning "measuring rod". Process of choosing books to be included in scripture.

Catechism   A structural form of formal catholic education on doctrine, theology and scripture, usually taught as a course.

Catharsis   A process of cleansing or purification with an individual becoming free from obstacles to catholic growth or progress.

Catholic   A term for the universal church, in contrast to forms and denominations of churches.

Christology	A section of theology focusing on the person of Jesus Christ; especially the dual natures of humanity and deity.
Covenant	Agreement.
Creed	A formal writing of faith beliefs; generally unique to denominations.
Decalogue	The Ten Commandments.
Docetism	An early heresy that saw Jesus as being totally divine with only the appearance of being human.
Ecclesiology	The docrine or theology of the church.
Eschatology	The theology of the "end times."
Exegesis	Textual study and interpretation of scripture.
Fourth Gospel	The book of John which is different in many ways from the synoptic gospels of Matthew, Mark and Luke.
Fundamentalism	A legalistic take on faith and scripture in which a literal and conservative view is regularly adopted.
Gnosticism	A system of religious thought in which the Acquisition of Knowledge is paramount; knowledge is often seen as only for the chosen or initiated.
Grace	Unmerited favor; a gift; a pardon.

Incarnation	The assumption of a human nature by Jesus Christ; Jesus became flesh.
Immanuel	Literally, "God with us."
Justification	Christ's sacrifice "justifies" the believer in relation to the wrongs of the sin condition.
Liturgy	A written text or set forms of worship.
Logos	Greek term for meaning "word."
Meditation	A form of prayer or thought in which the individual uses images to focus on God.
Messiah	Literally "Anointed One."
Modalism	A heresy of the Trinity; views God as one person who assumes roles or modes as needed thoughout time.
Monotheism	Belief or faith in one God.
Orthodoxy	Right belief; seen in contrast to obvious bad theology or doctrine.
Orthopraxis	Right practice, or actions or application.
Pantheism	Belief or faith in multiple gods.
Paraclete	Advocate; used by John to describe the Holy Spirit post-resurrection of Jesus.

Parousia	Greek term literally meaning "coming" or "arrival"; normally refers to the second coming of Christ.
Pneumatological	Doctrine of the Holy Spirit.
Praxis	Greek term literally meaning "action" also used to define practice or application.
Sacrament	A rite instituted by Jesus, now primarily observed in worship; Protestants practice two — baptism and communion (Lord's Supper).
Soteriological	Theology of Salvation.
Synoptic Gospels	Greek word for "summary" used to describe the common writings of Matthew, Mark and Luke.
Telos	Greek word for "end" or "purpose."
Theocentric	Centered on God.
Theophanies	Appearance of God or the divine.
Torah	Jewish/Hebrew Law.
Trinity	Theology of God as three distinct persons of God, Jesus and Holy Spirit.

Made in the USA
Charleston, SC
19 March 2014